The Development of Gymnastic Skills

The Development of Gymnastic Skills

A SCHEME OF WORK FOR TEACHERS

M. D. TREVOR

Physical Education Inspector, Nottinghamshire

BASIL BLACKWELL · OXFORD

0 631 12577 9

Designed and typeset in 12pt Palatino by Oxprint Ltd
Printed by The Camelot Press Limited, Southampton
and bound by James Burn Eynsham Limited

Contents

Foreword

This book explains in the simplest terms how to teach gymnastics to children along educational rather than formal lines. The approach described is probably the easiest to understand and for many teachers the most effective.

Forty units of work are presented and, because each item of each unit is different, there are about two hundred activities placed as far as possible in a reasonably logical sequence. This should provide the basis for a scheme of work over a number of years and ensure some continuity through the school. There will clearly be need for a great deal of repetition and, as the children proceed through the scheme, many items will be carried forward from one lesson to another. The teacher will also be able to add his own tried and tested work.

This is not a scheme to be followed meticulously and laboriously, but one which is readily available as an instant aid. For this reason the problems are worded exactly as the teacher may speak to the class.

This is intended to be a working book—one that you put in your pocket or stand up on the piano. It is the book which instantly reminds you what you did in the last lesson and provides the basis of the next.

With this in mind, the book has been designed to leave space for teachers to make their own notes at appropriate points.

Teaching Method

Setting the problems

The children are set a physical problem in deliberately simple terms, which they are then able to interpret at various levels according to their ability. For instance, the problem:

'Balance on three parts of your body.'

may be translated by one child into a simple balance involving two feet and one hand, or by another into a more difficult balance using two hands and the head.

Most problems will be phrased using a combination of the following words:

stretch
jump
curl
twist
balance
points
roll
weight (on different parts of the body).

Added to these words may be:

over
under
through
around

which give some idea of direction, particularly when using apparatus.

And, finally:

fast
slow

to indicate changes of speed. Other words are, of course, used, but these are the main ones.

The early problems which are set should be short and simple, for example:

'Find three different ways of rolling.'
'Balance on three points of the body.'
(This usually means a combination of hands, knees, feet, elbows or head.)
'Jump with a stretch.
'Over with a weight on hands.'

It is much easier for the children to understand this approach if, in the first stages, these tasks are set using the floor only. Introducing too much apparatus too soon confuses not only the children, but also the teacher, and often results in a lesson which degenerates into aimless clambering. Static balance positions should be held for only a few seconds.

Within a few lessons, movements or shapes may be linked together to form simple sequences of two movements, for example:

'Make a curled shape which shoots out quickly into a stretch .'
'Join together two different jumps.'
'Weight on hands, followed by a roll.'

Later, three or more movements or balances may be linked together, for example:

'Leap. Weight on hands. Roll.'
'Over with a stretch. Roll. Balance on three points.'

Changes of speed or direction may also be suggested.

At the same time apparatus may be gradually introduced. Simple problems are set which allow the children a great deal of freedom and give plenty of time for them to gain confidence. Eventually, these may evolve into sequences such as:

'Over the apparatus with a stretch. Weight on hands on the floor. Roll on the mat.'

which obviously require the children to use the floor, the mats and the apparatus in one sequence, an important point when the full use of the hall or gymnasium is necessary because of large numbers of children or a shortage of equipment.

A point often forgotten is that most children involved in gymnastic movement will never actually see themselves in action. The footballer will see when he has made a good pass and be overjoyed when his shot hits the roof of the net. The gymnast, however, may have only a vague feeling that he has done well and will almost certainly look to the teacher for some reaction. It is, therefore, vital that teachers show their reactions in a positive way. In some respects the teacher is taking the place of a mirror into which the children look for assurance. Reactions must, therefore, reflect the work being done.

What to look for

Having set the problem and ensured that the children are using all of the available space, look for variety in the way in which the problem is being solved. For example, if the problem set is:

'Find different ways of balancing on three points.'

most children will produce a balance which involves variations of hands and feet touching the floor. A good technique at this stage is to allow one half of the class to sit and watch the oth·r half work. The children should be asked to look for those children who have found an unusual way of solving the problem. It will become obvious quite quickly that elbows, knees or head might also be used. This method of putting half of the class under observation is important, in that the children are shown a variety of solutions, and in that those who are less able may see children of similar ability amongst the demonstrators. The over-use of very able children in individual demonstrations is something to be avoided.

Sometimes, in order to achieve more variety and movement, a further limitation to the original problem may need to be added. For example, the problem:

'Moving in lots of different ways.'

may result in the usual running, hopping, skipping and jumping, etc, but, if it is obvious that all these movements involve travelling in a forward direction, the teacher may add:

'Now find ways of moving sideways.'

or perhaps:

'Moving—using three points.'

The teacher who persists in this pursuit of variety is likely to see his children progress very rapidly.

Use of apparatus

In general it would seem sensible to progress from lessons requiring no apparatus (floor lessons) to those which require simple apparatus (benches, mats, etc) and then, later, to full apparatus lessons (benches, mats, trestles, stools and fixed apparatus and other tubular apparatus). In practice, because floor lessons offer so much scope for gymnastic work, a time will be reached when floor lessons and apparatus lessons may alternate.

It is important to note that in 'apparatus lessons' much of the work will involve the floor, for example:

'Show me a three-point balance which has two points touching the floor and one touching the apparatus.'
'On and off the apparatus with a stretch.'
'Using the apparatus, over with a stretch, followed by a weight on hands on the floor.'

This combination of floor and apparatus work provides the space for movements to flow. The type of problem which is phrased in such a way that the solution can be found only *on* the apparatus will sometimes result in static work because of overcrowding.

Class organization using apparatus

There are several methods.

1 Set out the apparatus. Set the same problem for the whole class and allow them to move about quite freely, trying to find solutions on many different kinds and levels of apparatus.

8

This method allows the children to choose the apparatus which suits their ability. The organization is very simple, and because all the children are concerned with the same problem, any form of demonstration or teaching point is relevant to every child. This approach requires the apparatus to be set out in such a way that no one piece or combination dominates, thereby causing overcrowding. The sensible use of space on and off the apparatus must be emphasised.

2 Set out the apparatus. Set the same problem for all the children, but place them in groups and limit each group to a set combination of apparatus.

This method lends itself to an orderly use of apparatus without overcrowding. After a reasonable amount of time, groups will move to another piece of apparatus. While waiting to start, children should sit round their apparatus in a pattern. This will suggest that the apparatus may be approached from many different angles rather than from a single direction—which is often the case when children line up before starting.

3 Set out the apparatus in such a way that specific combinations of apparatus favour certain types of activity. Place the children in groups and limit them to a specific problem on their combination of apparatus. For example:

Group 1 Two box tops and one bench.
'On and off fast with a stretch.'

Group 2 Two trestles and one ladder.
'Find three different swinging movements.'

This method is often used by specialist teachers in physical education at secondary school level. It is a sensible approach where apparatus is available which suggests more specialised use.

Most primary school teachers will favour an approach which is a combination of the first two methods, but much will depend upon the amount of equipment available and the size of the hall.

The activities suggested here are suitable for all three methods of apparatus work.

The use of mats in educational gymnastics

A mat is a valuable piece of gymnastic apparatus in its own right. It is less often used in educational gymnastics as a safety mat. Clearly, if children are encouraged to experiment and find out for themselves, there will be, in most cases, no clearly defined entry and exit point of a piece of apparatus and therefore the accurate positioning of a mat for safety purposes is not possible. Mats are usually placed in the spaces between apparatus. In general, the placing of mats at the end of apparatus is to be avoided as it suggests to the children a set direction in which the apparatus should be used.

9

If we consider the sequence in this problem:

> 'Using the apparatus, over with a stretch, followed by a weight on hands on the floor, then a roll on a mat.'

the mat being used will be some distance from the apparatus.

The use of mats for safety purposes

Where an activity has been phrased in such a way that the interpretation is reasonably predictable and perhaps a landing point from some height is indicated, then it is sensible to use a mat at that point. However, this mat must provide a firm grip on the floor. A slippery mat is more dangerous than no mat at all. Mats with a smooth texture on the under side grip quite well initially—but, unfortunately, tend to pick up polish from the floor and eventually provide a hazardous landing surface.

A few activities will benefit from having a mat close by. For example, a tubular bar at waist height suggests circling and balancing movements which may be followed by a roll on the mat—from experience this becomes predictable. Fortunately, children rarely fall from a dangerous height. One of the benefits of the educational gymnastics approach is that timid children are unlikely to be high up in the first place. Some teachers prefer to place mats under particularly high pieces of apparatus, which may well give them peace of mind, but, unfortunately, the location of a falling accident can be very unpredictable.

Setting out apparatus

An area which has been set out for apparatus work should, in general, look balanced. Experienced teachers will often automatically leave the centre of the area open, thus allowing for freedom of movement across the hall or gymnasium and also unrestricted observation.

Where a combination of apparatus is to be linked, it is advisable to consider placing it in L shapes or other combinations. Apparatus fixed in a straight line suggests that it should be used in that direction. In the early stages of apparatus work children tend to follow the line of the apparatus and a 'follow-the-leader' situation develops. The observant teacher will ask for movements which cross the line of apparatus. Apparatus linked at right angles usually has more stability.

Storage and movement of equipment

A school hall normally has a large number of different uses, and storage of equipment will inevitably cause problems. Many schools have PE stores, but from the point of view of putting out large gymnastic equipment it is often more convenient to store it against the walls of the hall. Certainly the untangling of trestles, ladders, stools, etc, from a confined space can be frustrating, and sometimes sufficiently off-putting to reduce its use seriously.

Ideally, equipment should be set out by the children. This requires careful instruction and many would say that this in itself is good social training. Some schools choose to set out apparatus for certain blocks of time, when it can be used by several classes. Under these circumstances, it is important to adjust the equipment to suit the various classes. In some instances this may require only the alteration of linkage heights or perhaps the complete removal of linking apparatus.

How to use the forty units of work

Each unit forms the basis of one or more lessons. The units are placed in order of difficulty and, therefore, the first question is where to start. Where it is clear that little work has been covered in the past, the obvious starting point is unit one. The age of the children at this point is not particularly relevant, since this type of work demands interpretation by the children, which may be at many levels. For example, item B in Unit 1 asks:

'Balance on any part of your body.'

This may legitimately be asked of an infant, junior or secondary child. The only difference will be in the variety and level of work which emerges. More able children in the school may require a later starting point.

Work involving various types of apparatus is introduced gradually. Some teachers may decide to bring this forward a little, but still to keep it in order.

Units involving floor and mat work continue alongside those concerned with apparatus work. Those teachers who prefer lessons which start with a clear floor, and end with apparatus work, will be able to combine these units.

Many of the early units are illustrated by examples of work which the teachers might expect to see, and, because this is intended as a working scheme, there is also space for the teachers' notes. It is a good idea to record alternative ways of phrasing a task—sometimes the mere alteration of a word will bring a more understanding or varied response from the children. A quick 'matchstick man' type of drawing is also a useful aid to the memory. As the units progress and the tasks become more complicated, illustrations become less appropriate and are gradually phased out.

A. Running about in lots of different directions. Change direction each time I say, 'Change'.

Children will usually run all in the same direction until you emphasise running across the hall and towards corners, etc. Emphasise no touching. Give praise to those who dodge well.

B. Balance on any part of your body. Make your shape different from anyone else's in the class.

Look for balances on bottoms, tummy, one foot and, perhaps, top of back and shoulders. Give praise for new ideas. Use half class demonstration.

C. Moving about in a lot of different ways. (*Hopping, running, jumping, etc.*) Alter the way you are moving each time I say, 'Change'.

Emphasise no touching. After about four changes children will have to think about bunny hops, rolling and movements which go backwards and sideways.

D. Balance with three parts of your body touching the floor. Find lots of different ways.

Look for original ideas, e.g., back of head, knees or perhaps elbows. Use half class demonstration. Involve the children who are observing in helping you to spot good ideas.

E. Moving about the floor using hands and feet.

Expect to see variations on bunny jumps, early stages of cartwheels (legs bent), running on all fours. Look for variety.

A. Moving about in lots of different ways. Change direction each time I say, 'Change'. If I say, 'Backwards', try to do the movement backwards. (*Add 'sideways', 'backwards' and 'turning'.*)

Children will normally 'follow their noses' when given a choice of movement. By adding words such as 'backwards', 'sideways' or 'turning' you will ensure more variety.

B. Moving about using three parts of your body . . . two parts . . . four parts. (*Add 'sideways', 'turning', 'backwards'.*)

In the early stages this normally results in various ways of using hands and feet.

C. Put your hands on the floor and kick your feet in the air. Stay with your weight on your hands for as long as possible. Make different shapes with your legs before they come down.

Discuss what 'weight on hands' means. Fingers should point forwards on the floor. Children will kick higher if the nose is positioned in front of the fingers.

D. Standing, jump as high as you can, flinging up your arms. Make any shape in the air.

It is important that children throw their arms upwards when attempting to jump high.

E. Run three or four steps and jump very high.

Children usually run far too fast when attempting to jump high. Limit the number of steps. One- or two-footed take off. Emphasise the use of the arms on take off.

A. Running about in lots of different directions—show sudden changes in speed.

Emphasise the difference between a slow jogging run and a sudden darting movement. The fast stage need last only about four or five steps.

B. Weight on hands. Try to count up to three before your legs come down. Make different shapes with your legs.

Legs very straight or legs bent fully at the knees or, perhaps, legs wide astride, etc. Emphasise nose in front of hands before kicking upwards.

C. Moving about in lots of different ways, show sudden changes of speed.

Some movements are easier than others to speed up, e.g. walking, running, hopping.

D. Find three different ways of jumping sideways. (*Standing jump.*)

Two feet on to one foot, tall shape to small shape, crouching jump sideways into a stretched shape, etc.

E. Curl up small. Shoot out quickly into a stretched shape.

Initially, most children will jump up into a standing stretch. Many shapes supported on various parts of the body are also stretched shapes. Some children may take up stretched shapes on the floor.

A. Run with changes of speed and direction
. . . add sudden stops.

*This is really an exercise in the use of all available space.
Say, 'The good ones are those who can spot the spaces first
and dart into them!'*

B. Crouch down. Put your hands flat on the floor
with your fingers pointing forwards. Have your
hands about as wide apart as your shoulders.
Kick up in the air with your feet. Move about
doing this.

*These are really 'bunny jumps'. Look for legs which kick
high in the air. It is a good idea to add, 'Now keep your legs
curled up tight and think about getting your bottom high
in the air.'*

C. Find three different ways of jumping backwards. (*Standing jumps*).

*Tall shape to small. Small to tall. Two feet on to one foot,
etc.*

D. Balance on your bottom. Make any shapes by
moving your arms and legs into different
positions. Choose one of these shapes and,
without overbalancing, move slowly on to your
hip.

*Indicate where the hips are—many children do not know!
Balances of this kind are quite difficult. You should expect
a balance of only a few seconds' duration.*

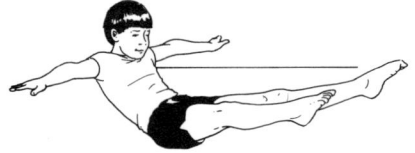 

E. Curl up small. Shoot out quickly into a stretched shape—back slowly into a curl. Roll somewhere. Repeat.

Look for a definite change in speed. The rolls will be quite simple ones at this stage. Some of the stretched shapes may be supported on varied combinations of hands, feet, knees, etc. Even at this stage, you should be looking for movements which are linked smoothly and with control.

A. Run quickly. Jump high and land without losing control. Make different shapes in the air. Land with your feet apart and arms spread wide.

Emphasise landing with feet apart and arms spread wide to help balance.

B. Find ways of balancing with your weight on your hands.

Accept any position where hands are on the floor and the rest of the body is off the floor. Most children will manage balances for only a few seconds. Use half class demonstration for ideas. Ideally, balances do not wobble.

C. Run three or four steps, jump high and make any stretched shape in the air.

Children often run too quickly. Slow them down. Emphasise controlled landings with feet apart.

D. Balance on your back. Make many shapes by moving arms and legs into different positions. Now curl and then shoot your arms out into different positions. Repeat.

Perhaps suggest that, while the children are curled, they roll away and repeat as they arrive on their backs again.

E. Balance on your bottom. Curl. Roll away and come out into a balance on your back. Curl and repeat.

This is similar to problem D.

F. Three standing jumps. See how far you can travel.

Emphasise a big swing of the arms to help gain distance.

18

A. Run three or four steps. Jump high and make a curled shape in the air.

Arms must be thrown in the air for height. Land with feet apart. This is quite difficult. Accept landings with body still in the crouch position.

B. Run three or four steps. Jump high, turn in the air and land facing the way you came from.

On landing, arms should be stretched forwards, to counteract the tendency to fall backwards. Landings with feet apart.

C. Find ways of balancing on three points. (*Discuss points at this stage.*)

Two hands, two feet, two elbows, two knees plus head are the nine points of the body which you are looking for. These are small areas, as opposed to larger areas, such as the back, bottom, tummy and shoulders.

D. Curl. Shoot out quickly into a three-point balance. Repeat several times, coming out into different three-point balances each time.

Emphasise the speed of the movement.

E. Run three or four steps. Jump high and make any stretched shape with a turn in the air.

Usually the children will produce symmetrical shapes, more often than not resembling star shapes.

A. Moving about on hands and feet, keeping arms and legs straight.

Most children will 'follow their noses'. Encourage sideways and backwards movements.

B. Find different ways of rolling on the floor. (*Without mats.*)

If children try to roll backwards, tell them to roll over one shoulder rather than directly over their heads.

C. Balance on your stomach (tummy). Make many shapes by moving arms and legs into different positions.

Spend only a short time on this. This type of balance is limited but very strenuous.

D. Free running and jumping. Go for distance or height.

You should be able to recognize the difference. Concentrate on quiet, controlled landings. Once again, children who are trying for height often run too quickly.

E. Balance on your shoulders (and the top of your back). Make many shapes by moving your arms and legs into different positions. Now move from a balance on your tummy to a balance on your shoulders

Feet and hands should not touch the floor.

F. Find ways of balancing on three points. If you have an arm or a leg which you are not using, stretch it out.

Emphasise pointed toes, fingers together. The shapes achieved should then become considerably more pleasing. Let half the class demonstrate while the other half looks for original ideas.

20

A. Run three or four steps, jump high and make any shape in the air, but land in a curled shape. Land very quietly.

Ensure a short run up. Use of arms to obtain height.

B. Balance on any parts of the body, curl, roll and come out quickly into another balance. Repeat the sequence.

In the first stages 'talk' the children through, so that all the children are working to your timing. Then allow them to work in their own time.

C. From a standing position, join together two different jumps in a straight line.

This may involve a change of body shape. Eventually, ask for the two jumps to be performed without a pause.

D. Weight on hands with legs in curled shapes.

Nose in front of fingers. Bottom as high as possible before kicking up. Hands shoulder-width apart.

E. With a partner, make a bridge shape with your body. Allow your partner to slide underneath without touching you. He must then make a bridge and you move smoothly under him.

This is the first of the partner activities. Stress not touching. Emphasise being careful with each other.

A. Moving about on two points . . . three points
. . . four points.

*Then add 'backwards', which means moving in whatever
way has been decided, but backwards. Similarly with
'sideways'. Unless you add these limitations children will
usually move only forwards.*

B. Move from a balance on your back to a balance
on your stomach (tummy), without touching the
floor with other points (hands, feet, knees,
elbows, head).

*Hands and feet should not touch the floor. As this is a
strong activity, do not persist too long.*

C. From a standing position, join together two
different jumps. Change direction with the
second jump.

*In the first stages the children will pause between each
jump. You are really looking for two consecutive jumps
without a pause.*

D. Move smoothly from one balanced shape to
another. Stretch arms and legs in each balance.

*Encourage the children to link balances which are very
different, e.g., a balance on the bottom, a balance on three
points and a balance on one foot.*

E. Practise any weight on hands activity. Try to
count up to five while your legs are in the air.

A. From a standing position, join together three different jumps in a straight line.

E.g., One foot on to two feet, stretched shapes, curled shapes.

B. Weight on hands, with legs in stretched shapes.

Usually this results in kicking upwards into something like a handstand.

C. Walk towards spaces and do a moving weight on hands.

Children should walk confidently into spaces, performing a weight on hands on the move about every four or five steps, without touching anyone. Children tend to move into a circle. Emphasise working in every available space—use corners.

D. Run quickly with sudden changes of direction. Sometimes stop completely before setting off again.

Encourage confident controlled running. Say, 'If you are good at this you will never touch anyone—not even brush past them!' Children will naturally run in large looping circles. Emphasise strongly the suddenness of the change of direction.

E. With a partner. Make a bridge shape with your body. Allow your partner to go underneath without touching. Then he must make a bridge. Make a different bridge each time it is your turn.

Ideally, there is a flow of movement here, e.g., as a child sees that his partner has passed under him he starts to move towards his partner's bridge. There is often a snake-like quality about this activity.

A. Run three or four steps and jump very high with a turn in the air. Land with feet apart.

Look for quiet, controlled, landings, with feet apart, i.e., children should not stagger backwards before stopping.

B. Balance on three points in such a way that your right foot is the highest part of your body. Find a number of balances like this.

Use half class demonstration for ideas. Knees, elbows and the back of the head are the points which are often forgotten.

Mats out

C. Moving in lots of different ways. When you come to a mat, roll on it. Try to have rolled on each mat before we stop.

Spread the mats evenly around the hall, but not necessarily in any sort of pattern. Explain that it is possible for two children to use one mat at the same time—particularly with mats 6ft × 4ft—provided they work across the width. Emphasise no touching each other.

D. Walk around, practising weight on hands on the floor. When you come to a mat, roll on it. Now try to make your weight-on-hands activity finish near a mat, so that you can go straight into a roll.

You are looking for smooth linkage between the weight on hands and the roll. The children move around freely, using all the mats. About 8 mats per 30 children is sufficient.

E. Run anywhere, dodge each other, jump over mats or the corner of mats. Do not touch the mats with your feet. Now, as you jump over the mats, turn in the air to land facing the mat.

Light landings. Toes touching the floor before heels. Give at the knees. Land with feet apart.

A. Run three or four steps. Jump high with a stretched shape. Land in a curled shape.

Some children may be able to produce asymmetrical shapes. Jumps must be high in order to give sufficient time for a change of shape. Symmetry is worth discussing here with older children.

B. Crouch down. Kick up into a weight on hands and notice where your feet are when they come down. Imagine you have white paint on the soles of your feet. Each time your feet come down, try to make footprints in different places.

Ask for a weight on hands where the feet stay a long time in the air before coming down. Head well forward before kicking up. This activity should add more variety to the childrens' work.

Mats out

C. Sit with your group in a pattern round your mat. Perform simple rolls in such a way that the mat is always in use.

This is an attempt to use the mat without queueing. Encourage the children to use as little of the mat as possible, i.e. to roll across the width or corners. Ideally no more than 4 children to a mat.

D. Sit round your mat and find three different ways of rolling in a curled shape.

Three methods—simply forwards, backwards or sideways.

E. Walking around using all the mats. Weight on hands on the mats—but do not let your feet come down on to the mat.

The children will often need to stretch their legs out in their attempts to avoid the mats with their feet. Eventually, ask the children to turn and finish facing the mat.

25

A. Walking. Weight on hands with feet coming down into different positions. Walk towards spaces. Kick feet as high as possible.

Ask for such things as 'feet landing close to hands'; 'feet landing well away from hands'; 'one foot close to hands, the other well away'.

B. Run three or four steps, leap high with a stretch and a turn. Land in a curled shape.

Use of arms. Do not run quickly.

C. Sit down. Legs straight (either together or apart). Find ways of standing up without bending your legs.

Cross legs over in a scissor-like action to face the floor, push up with hands into a standing position with feet apart. Some may think of rolling backwards over the head or over one shoulder and pushing into standing position.

Mats out

D. Running anywhere, jump over the mats but land facing them. If the mat is clear, roll on it. Use all the mats.

A class of thirty needs eight mats or more. Controlled landing, with arms forward to stop the tendency to over-balance backwards, and feet apart.

E. Roll on the mat nearest to you. Walk to another mat and roll in a different way. And so on.

On the largest mats two children may roll at the same time. Use half class to show variety.

F. Sit in groups round the mats. Find three different ways of rolling with legs staying perfectly straight. Now roll with straight legs and then stand up with straight legs.

This problem is well worth persisting with. It can result in elegant movements with a recognizable gymnastic style. If feet are kept well apart after a forward roll some children may be able to stand without bending their legs. Remind children of item C in this unit.

A. From a standing position, join together three different jumps travelling in the direction of a triangle.

In the first stages the children will pause between each jump in order to give themselves thinking time. Eventually ask for three continuous jumps.

B. Balance on one of your hips. Make many shapes by moving arms and legs into different positions.

This is a difficult balancing position with limited solutions. Do not persist for long.

C. Crouch down. Weight on hands, with feet landing in such a way that they point away from your hands. Now repeat at walking speed.

Most weight-on-hands activities finish with feet pointing towards hands. This problem requires that the children twist at the waist as they come down. They perform either an inward twist or an outward twist.

Mats out

D. Stand five or six strides away from a mat. With a short run, leap high with a turn in the air. Follow with a roll on the mat.

Let the children move around freely, using all the mats. When they have found a good sequence, suggest that they stay on the same mat and perfect it. This particular sequence is one of the simplest and yet one of the most effective and is well worth persisting with.

E. Stand with your group round your mat and about three good strides away from it. Do a weight on hands on the floor which you can follow smoothly with a roll on the mat.

Children will usually stand too close to the mats for this sequence. The weight on hands must be on the floor and not on the mat.

F. Make a three-point balance on the mat. Slowly change this balance into a roll.

Remind the children about backward rolls.

A. From a standing position, join together four different jumps, travelling in the direction of a square.

Allow a pause between each jump in the early stages. Expect jumps linked together continuously later.

B. Weight on hands—move one hand and then bring the feet down in a different place.

This is really the first stage of a hand walk. Legs should be as high in the air as possible.

C. Weight on hands—walk two steps on hands before your feet come down.

The main fear children have when kicking up high into any weight on hands is that they will go right over the top and land on their backs. This might be a good time to point out that by lifting, say, your right hand off the floor your body will come down on that side. This is a good safety factor and should be explained.

Mats out

D. Sit in a group around your mats. Find three different ways of rolling sideways.

Usually children will roll in a curled shape or a stretched shape (like a rolling pin). Occasionally a child may produce a 'cartwheel'—accept this.

E. Any kind of roll on the mat. Come smoothly out of this roll into a three-point balance. Hold the balance for three seconds.

Emphasise the smooth linkage between the roll and the balance. Most balances will be of the type where the child ends up facing the floor. It is possible to finish looking at the ceiling.

F. Try to perform a roll which changes direction about half way through the movement.

Usually a roll follows the direction of a straight line. It may help to chalk a line on the mat when explaining.

Box tops, benches, low stools, stage-blocks scattered evenly about the hall. Mats placed in the spaces and not next to apparatus.

A. Jumping carefully from apparatus to land softly and with control. Walk from one piece of apparatus to another. Roll on the mats—try jumping from different heights.

Use of arms for balance. Landing toes first, feet apart, give at the knees. N.B. These landings should be on the floor and not on the mats. Emphasise continuous movement. No one should need to wait for a go and no one should touch anyone else.

B. Over the apparatus with a weight on hands. Walk to another piece of apparatus. Use the mats for rolling as you move about.

This simply involves putting the hands on any part of the apparatus and passing over that part with the weight supported by the hands. Sometimes it is possible to pass over the apparatus by using a weight on hands on the floor, e.g. over a bench.

C. Three-point balances. Two of the points must be touching the apparatus and one touching the floor. Try this on several pieces of apparatus.

After a while you will probably have to stress the use of elbows, knees and head.

D. Off with a stretch. Use mats for rolls as you change from one piece of apparatus to another.

Often this will be interpreted as jumping off with arms and legs straight. It could also mean coming off with a weight on hands in a stretched shape.

E. Free practice, using any of the activities which you have just been doing. Keep moving. Do not touch anyone.

You should see a good range of activity now. Emphasise strongly continuous activity without touching.

Box tops, benches, low stools, stage-blocks scattered evenly about the hall. Mats placed in the spaces and not next to apparatus.

A. On and off the apparatus with a jump. Land softly and with control. Use the mats for rolling backwards as you change to another piece of apparatus.

Accept rolls which go over one shoulder.

B. Jump off the apparatus with a stretch.

Point out the differences between symmetrical and asymmetrical shapes—the latter are far more difficult.

C. Over the apparatus with a weight on hands. Stretch your legs out as you go over. Use the mats for rolling.

Emphasise the straight legs and pointed toes. Expect to see a variety of rolls on the mats.

D. Three-point balances—two points touching the floor and one point touching the apparatus. If you have one arm or a leg which you are not using, stretch it out. Use the mats for rolls with straight legs.

Ask for real effort with the parts being stretched and this work can look most effective. Let one half watch the others to look for original work.

E. Off the apparatus with a jump. Make a curled shape before you land. Try to land near a mat and then roll on it.

You may have to move some of the mats closer to the apparatus (about 2 metres away).

F. Try to join together a jump, a roll and a three-point balance.

The jump is from the apparatus.

*Box tops, benches, stools, stage-blocks, trestles, etc,
scattered evenly about the hall. Mats in spaces. Trestles
not linked to other apparatus.*

A. Moving freely on and off the apparatus. Do not
wait for a go. Do not touch anyone. Use mats for
rolling.

*We have now introduced the trestles into the apparatus
set-out and it is important that children are taught to
move freely without touching anyone and without
waiting for a go. Discourage any signs of queueing.*

B. Free moving without touching anyone.
Wherever you are, when I say, 'Stretch', make a
safe, stretching shape.

*The children hold these shapes for only a few seconds and
then continue free moving.*

C. Free moving without touching anyone.
Wherever you are, when I say, 'Curl', make a
curled shape.

The results will be more limited than the above problem.

D. One and off quickly with a stretch.

*This problem does not allow for any climbing to the tops of
trestles, etc. Ask the children to pretend the apparatus is
hot, in order to produce quick on/off movement.*

E. Move about the apparatus, going from stretch to
curl, stretch to curl. Try to move as far as
possible.

*Children must avoid each other by twisting and turning
round other bodies. No touching is allowed. Keep strictly
to clear-cut curls and stretches—no walking.*

*Box tops, benches, stools, stage-blocks, trestles, etc,
scattered evenly. Mats away from apparatus. Trestles not
linked to other apparatus.*

A. Free climbing on the apparatus. Do not stand
behind anyone and wait for a go. Everyone must
keep moving.

*Eliminate any queues which form. Perhaps show a trestle
being used by five or six children attempting to move
without touching. A very important teaching point is
concern for other children's safety by not touching.*

B. Free moving about the apparatus. When I say,
'Stop', make an interesting shape with your
right foot the highest part of your body. Try to
make your shape the only one like it in the class.

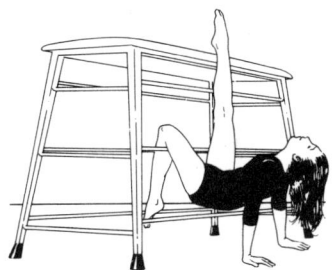

*Not many children will think of a shape where they are
facing the ceiling.*

C. Using the apparatus. Over with a curl.

*This problem also applies to the mats. Various bars lend
themselves to this problem.*

D. Upside-down stretched shapes, using the
apparatus. Try this, using various pieces of
apparatus.

*This may result in variations on a handstand on the floor,
using the apparatus for support. For those children who
do not usually go very high with weight on hands, this
can be a valuable practice.*

E. Jump off the apparatus, turn in the air and land
facing the apparatus. Land with your feet apart.
Now, if you are able to land near a mat, follow
with a roll.

This is obviously likely to be a backward roll.

A. Run quickly. Join together two different leaps. Cover as much ground as possible.

In a small hall you may have to control the direction in which the children run, e.g., the running and jumping in one direction down the centre of the hall and the return close to the walls.

B. Weight on hands. Try to walk several steps with legs curled.

Nose well forward. Bottom high before kicking up. (See Unit 15 C for safety factor).

C. Running—weight on hands with feet landing in different positions.

Feet landing together, apart, pointing away from hands, etc. When children are concentrating on the position of their feet, they often forget to land lightly. They may also tend to run too quickly for good control, so slow them down.

Mats out

D. Find five different ways of rolling. Work in groups, each using one mat.

E. Stand with your group round your mat and about three good strides away from it. Do a weight on hands which will enable you to follow it smoothly with a roll on the mat. Stand up using straight legs.

Ideally the weight on hands will finish with feet next to mat.

A. Run quickly. Join together three different jumps. Cover as much ground as possible.

Control the direction of running, if using a small area.

B. Weight on hands. Try to walk several steps with legs stretched.

The children will not be able to walk far until they can kick one foot above and beyond their head. Allow the children to kick up against any spare walls.

C. Find five different three-point balances in which your head is always one of three points.

Use half class demonstration.

Mats out

D. Stand about eight good strides away from your mat. From a very short run, try a leap, weight on hands, roll, in such a way that the roll takes place on the mat.

This means leap, land, into a weight on hands, land close to the mat, roll on it.

E. Roll with straight legs. Show a change of direction about half way through the roll.

Use chalk on the mat to show a change of direction.

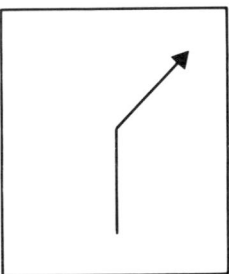

Apparatus out. Linked apparatus (bars, ladders, etc) at about one metre in height.

A. Free use of apparatus without touching anyone. Try to make lots of twisted shapes.

Emphasise continuous activity without touching. A twisted shape usually means twisted at the waist.

B. Free moving about the apparatus. When I say, 'Stop', make an interesting shape with your left shoulder the highest part of your body (or bottom the highest part of your body).

Look for unusual shapes.

C. Over with a stretch. Remember to use the mats also.

The children may choose any part of the apparatus, e.g., one of the bars on the trestle. Accept a movement where legs are straight but the rest of the body is perhaps curled. Benches offer many possibilities.

D. Use the apparatus to support you in doing a weight-on-hands balance on the floor.

The more able children may require only to touch the apparatus with one foot in order to maintain balance. The less able may require much more support, e.g., working inside a trestle.

E. Get on to the apparatus by using a weight on hands on the floor.

More often than not children will step on to the apparatus. Therefore this problem is an interesting one. One easy interpretation is a bunny hop on the floor with feet landing on a bench. Some may do a handstand or a similar movement up to a trestle, curl their legs round a bar and then pull upwards. Persist with this problem. It is important that children are able to connect movements on the floor with movements on the apparatus.

Apparatus out. Linked apparatus at about one metre high. Mats in spaces away from apparatus.

A. Use the apparatus freely. Do not stop moving. Try to use every piece of apparatus during the next three minutes. Practise your favourite movements.

You should by now see a variety of movement; at any time you should see bodies upright, horizontal, upside-down and in other various positions. If everyone appears to be spending most of the time upright, point it out and ask for variety.

B. Across a part of the apparatus with a curl and back across the same part with a stretch.

Mats may be neglected but they are a good piece of apparatus for this problem.

C. Free moving about the apparatus. When I say 'Stop', make an unusual shape with your right knee the highest part of your body (or tummy the highest part of your body).

This is a strenuous activity and balances should be held for only a few seconds.

Half class on apparatus

D. Find different parts of the body which may be used for hanging or swinging on the apparatus.

Half class using the mats away from the apparatus

E. Slow weight on hands on the floor, followed by a
fast roll on the mat.

*Swinging movements take up a great deal of space on the
apparatus and therefore it is better to split the class in this
way.*
Hanging from the back of the knees is not unusual.

Change around after a few minutes.

A. Walk three or four steps only, leap, turn and land on one foot. Balance.

This is difficult at anything faster than walking pace. Land with control and balance on one foot for a few seconds.

B. Curl—explode into a three-point balance. Slowly back into a curled shape. Roll. Repeat. Try to use several different types of balance.

Expect the children to cover at least half the length of the hall in this sequence. You should see a distinct change of speed during the sequence.

C. A slow weight on hands which goes into a slow roll and then explodes into a three-point balance.

Usually this means weight on hands, then landing before going into a roll. Occasionally you will see a child lower himself from the weight on hands and go directly into a roll without his feet touching the ground. This is much more difficult and is usually seen on mats.

Pairs

D. Help your partner to make any sort of balance— support him. When he is steady, change your shape slowly into another balance. You now have a pairs balance.

This is the first stage of working in pairs. Put great emphasis on the supporter's responsibility. Expect the children to talk to one another. Use half class demonstration. Look for variety.

Pairs

E. With a partner, make a pairs balance with only
one pair of feet between the two of you touching
the floor.

*This involves one child completely supporting another.
Say, 'Stretch out arms and legs not being used.' Expect
the children to become quite excited. Look for unusual
shapes. Usually the pair of feet touching the floor will be
quite wide apart to give a firm base.*

Apparatus out. Linked at about one metre high. Mats in spaces.

A. Curl on the apparatus, stretch quickly, and then pull or lower yourself slowly into another curl. Repeat. Show the difference in speed between the slow curl and the fast stretch.

Expect the children to cover some distance on the apparatus, rather than stay in one spot. The fast stretch is made after the child is sure that he will not touch anyone else.

B. Weight-on-hands balances on the apparatus. This is a shape which does not move, but all your weight is on your hands. Try this in lots of different parts of the apparatus.

The balance should be held for a few seconds only. Hanging by the hands is not a weight on hands.

Pairs

C. Work out a sequence of 'over, under and round' with your partner, using the apparatus. Try not to touch each other.

This should result in a controlled snake-like movement. It is likely to be slow and the emphasis is on not touching.

Pairs

D. Face your partner across a piece of apparatus and about two strides away from it. Make up a matching sequence with your partner which goes towards—on—off and then away from the apparatus in a straight line.

This is rather like moving towards and away from a mirror which is placed through the middle of the apparatus. Pairs of similar size and ability result in the best work.

46

A. Running slowly. Each time I clap my hands, change direction and sprint for about four paces; then slow down again.

This is a test of quick thinking and use of space.

B. Weight on hands. Walk on hands and count how many steps before your feet come down.

You should expect to see at least four steps even if the weight on hands is only a simple bunny hop. Children who are good at weight on hands might reach eight steps.

C. Balance on four points in such a way that your head is the highest part of your body. Find five different ways of doing this. Now the same thing with your left foot the highest point.

D. Balance on one point. Curl slowly. Roll. Explode into a two-point balance. Curl slowly. Roll. Explode into a three-point balance. Curl slowly, Roll. Explode into a four-point balance.

The balance should be still before starting the curl and roll again.

Pairs

E. Find five different ways of completely supporting your partner's weight. Try to make your combined shape different from that of any other pair in the class.

There is an enormous range of exciting possibilities here. Use half-class demonstrations.

Pairs

F. With a partner, make a combined shape with only two points touching the floor.

This often means one point per person touching the floor.

47

Apparatus out. Linked apparatus at about one metre high.
Mats in spaces

A. On to the apparatus, using weight on hands on
the apparatus.

Examples would be:
(a) Hands on bench. Kick up to weight on hands. Land
with feet on bench.
(b) Hands on bottom two bars of trestle. Kick up to hook
feet on higher bars.

B. Off the apparatus, using a weight on hands on
the floor.

This means directly off the apparatus into a weight on
hands on the floor, so that feet do not touch the floor until
after the weight on hands.

C. Weight on hands on the apparatus, followed by
a weight on hands on the floor.

We are now linking these first two problems. This is quite
difficult; therefore do not expect to see smooth linkage too
soon. This has been strong work so far and half-class
demonstrations would give a useful break.

D. Weight on hands on the apparatus. Weight on
hands on the floor, followed by a roll on a mat.

Make sure the mats are a suitable distance from the
apparatus. You may have to remind the children about
variations of rolls.

Pairs

E. Make a combined balance, with one partner on
the floor and the other on the apparatus.

Parts of the body not being used should be either fully
stretched or fully curled.

A. Run slowly and jump to the left or right with a change of direction.

This will need some coaching. Obviously, the faster the children run, the more difficult the movement becomes.

B. Weight-on-hands balances—all of your weight must be on your hands, with your body as still as possible.

Expect a balance to be held for about 4–5 seconds.

C. From a standing position find five ways of jumping backwards.

Curled position, leap backwards to stretched shape. Stretched shape, leap backwards to curled shape. Two feet, leap backwards to landing on one foot.

Pairs

D. With a partner, make a combined shape with only one back and one point touching the floor. Stretch out arms and legs which are not being used. Find several ways of doing this.

Pairs

E. With a partner, join together three different jumps which travel in a straight line. Perform this side by side and travelling in the same direction.

Pair off children of similar size and ability. The quality of the work will usually suffer while they concentrate on timing.

Pairs

F. As before, but following one behind the other and performing the jumps at the same time.

Apparatus out. Linked apparatus at various heights between one to two metres.

A. On and off fast, with a stretch. Turn in the air.

Contact with the apparatus for only a split second. Contact will usually be by feet but it could also be by hands and feet or hands only.

B. On and off fast, with a stretch. Turn in the air. Follow by a slow weight on hands.

This is a vigorous sequence. Emphasise care.

C. Pull mats towards the apparatus. Weight on hands supported by the apparatus. Lower slowly into a roll on the mats. Try this from a number of different positions.

The more able children may support their weight on hands by merely touching the apparatus with one foot. Some of the less able will still have to climb into an upside-down position. Remind the children that a wall, with a mat placed against it, can be used as supporting apparatus.

Push mats well away from apparatus
Half class using mats

D. Practise any kind of partner-supported balances away from apparatus. Find ways of lowering your partner into a roll—use the mats.

Half class using apparatus

E. Swinging movements on the apparatus. Make the movement as big as possible without losing control.

You may have to raise some of the linking bars, etc, for this activity. Some of the swinging movements may involve hanging by the legs.

Change

A. Running. Weight on hands with straight legs.

A cartwheeling action is likely to be the most popular. If there are any obvious straight lines on the floor (e.g., Badminton markings) suggest that the children stand with their feet apart and touching a line, move from there into a weight on hands on the same line, to their left or right, and then land with their feet touching the same line. This is one formal way of teaching a cartwheel.

B. Move from a shoulder balance, to a back balance, to a bottom balance, to a hip balance and then to a stomach (tummy) balance. Do not touch the floor with other points (hands, feet, knees, elbows, head).

This is strenuous. Do not persist for too long.

C. Balance on three points in such a way that your knee is the highest part of your body. Find several ways of doing this.

Most usual will be variations based on a 'crab' position.

D. Running quite quickly. Weight on hands, land on your feet; and then go straight into another weight-on-hands activity.

In a small area you will need to organize a one-way flow. Weight-on-hands activities at speed often result in cart-wheel-type actions.

Pairs

E. Pass over your partner's body with your weight on your hands on the floor.

Pairs

F. Put your weight on your hands and pass over your partner's body, placing your hands on your partner.

The easiest solution to this would be a leap-frog jump. There are many more difficult ones. The supporter must be in a very firm position, i.e., he must have a wide base in contact with the floor.

Mats placed in spaces.

A. Move over or through the apparatus with feet leading.

B. Over the apparatus slowly in a curl.

C. On to the apparatus with a jump. Off with a stretch.

D. On with a jump. Off with a stretch. Roll on a mat.

It is better to have the mats well away from the apparatus as this will extend the movements. Movements should not be 'telescoped' in order to fit in with badly positioned mats.

E. On with a jump. Off with a stretch. Roll on a mat. Stand up with straight legs.

When you build up a sequence of this kind, it is likely that the quality of each individual movement will suffer as the children concentrate on the linkage.

Half class using apparatus
Pairs

F. A swinging movement on the apparatus, where both of you are joined together.
Two examples would be:
(a) Hang by the arms. Link legs.
(b) Hang by the back of knees. Hold hands.

Half class using mats

G. Rolls in which hands do not touch the mat. Stand up without using hands.

Change

A. Join together with high leap with a turn in the air. Land and then go straight into a weight on hands.

B. Rocking or swaying. Make this movement larger and larger until it moves naturally into either a weight on hands or a roll.

Discuss the difference between rocking and swaying. In swaying, points are usually firmly fixed to the floor (as a tree sways). A rocking movement usually involves a movement of the points or area of contact with the floor (as with a rocking chair).

C. Crouch down. Jump very gently into a weight on hands. Try to leave the ground with your feet, before your hands touch the floor.

This is an unusual movement and it must be approached gently. It is rather like a bunny jump, where for a split second all of the body is off the floor. For those who manage this well, ask for variations of leg positions.

D. From a standing position, jump as high as possible to turn half way round. Land in a stretched shape. Repeat and land in a curled shape. See if you can turn further than this— and still land with control.

Some children will manage a complete 360° turn. Emphasise full control. Land with feet apart. Explain the use of arms to initiate the turn.

E. Place your hands on a line on the floor. Slow weight on hands with at least one foot landing on the other side of the line. Try with legs either straight or curled.

The child's body is working at right angles to the line.

Pairs

F. With a partner, make a combined shape with only one hand and one foot touching the floor.

Apparatus out. Children in pairs throughout the lesson.

A. Stand facing your partner across a piece of apparatus and about four strides from it. Make up a sequence of movements which takes you both forwards, on to the apparatus, off, and then back to your starting position. Both make the same movements, and try to keep in time with each other.

The children will do better if they keep the sequences simple in the first stages.

Half class on apparatus

B. In pairs. Link your body with your partner's. Make a combined swinging, rocking or swaying movement. Do not lose control with your partner. Now make this movement as big as possible without losing control.

Half class

C. In pairs. Same problem as for the other half of the class, but working on the floor or mats.

D. Make a combined balance with your partner in which two points are touching the floor and one point is touching the apparatus.

A. Join together five or six different jumps which take you in a zig-zag course.

With some children these jumps could be continuous.

B. Weight on hands as slowly as possible in a curled shape. Shoot legs out straight before they come down.

C. Crouch down. Leap as high as possible with a half turn or more and land in another crouch.

Some children will manage a full 360° turn.

D. Crouch and leap as before, trying to make a stretched shape before you land.

It is difficult to do this with a full turn.

E. Walking. Weight on hands. Push off with your hands so strongly that you feel as though your whole body is off the ground for a split second.

This is an attempt to develop a little bounce off the hands. It requires maximum effort in the push off with the hands.

Mats out

F. On the edge of the mat make a three-point balance which goes slowly into a roll.

Something which resembles the more formal headstand which overbalances into a roll is a common solution.

G. Any weight-on-hands activity on the mat, which lowers slowly into a roll.

Accept any weight-on-hands activity which goes directly into a roll, i.e., without the feet touching the floor between the movements.

57

Apparatus and mats equally spaced around the hall.

A. In fours. Starting about four paces from your apparatus, make up a sequence of movements which goes forwards, on, off, and back to your starting position. All four should keep in time. Choose simple movements to begin with.

Children will often choose movements which are far too complicated for good time-keeping.

Pairs

B. Find a way of coming off the apparatus, using your partner as a support.

The supporting partner must take up a strong position in order to take the weight.

Pairs

C. A pairs balance with one point touching the apparatus and one back touching the floor. Now do this in such a way that the top person lets go with the one point and is carefully supported to the floor.

Half class on apparatus

D. On to the apparatus using a slow weight on hands.

The children may use the floor or the apparatus for the weight on hands.

Half class on mats

E. Working across the corners of a mat, leap, roll, leap, roll sequence.

This sequence goes round on the mat in the direction of a rectangle. The rolls go across the corners and the leaps pass across the other corners.

A. Join together a number of three-point balances with simple rolls. Each balance should have a different part of the body for its highest point. Show a change of speed.

Because mats are not being used, many children will use sideways rolls or rolls which pass over one shoulder.

B. From a starting position. Weight on hands. Turn, using your hands, so that you face the place you came from.

C. Place both hands on a line. Weight on hands, with both feet landing the other side of the line.

D. Using the movements leap, weight on hands, roll, make up a sequence which carries you the farthest possible distance.

You could use mats for the roll part of the sequence.

E. Using any movements which you have learned in the past, make up a sequence which lasts about twenty seconds and shows a change of direction and a change of speed.

This exercise requires much thought and practice. It could well take up half the lesson and be repeated in several other lessons.

F. Run quite quickly. Leap and turn in the air to face the direction you came from. Land in a crouch position.

Throw arms forward on landing to counteract the tendency to overbalance backwards. Let the children now add any other movement to this activity.

Unit 37 *Full apparatus work*

A. Balance on two points—one point on the floor and one on the apparatus. Now make your hand the one point which is on the floor.

B. Make up a sequence which travels in a circle, involving the apparatus and the floor, and returns you to your starting point.

C. Move the mats close to spare walls or apparatus. Use the walls or the apparatus to enable you to do a weight on hands with straight legs. Lower into a roll and stand up with straight legs.

Those who find this easy might attempt problem D

D. Use the apparatus or the walls to get into a weight-on-hands position. From here walk on your hands to the nearest mat and lower into a roll.

A. Run quickly. Join three different jumps together. Try to cover as much distance as possible.

The hop, step and jump in athletics does this, but there are other combinations.

B. Walking. Weight on hands in such a way that for a split second the whole of your body is off the ground.

This is a gentle leap on to the hands. The arms must bend at the elbows to take the initial shock. Lead up to this slowly and carefully.

C. Choose any line on the floor. Stand with your feet apart and touching the line. Do a weight on hands in such a way that the points which touch the floor all travel along this line. Kick your legs as high as possible.

This will result in something which resembles a cart-wheel.

Pairs

D. Hold hands with a partner. Do not let go. Find out what sort of movements are possible. Are you able to roll?

Look for a wide range of solutions, e.g., running, jumping, balances, turning, supported balances.

Pairs

E. Face each other about eight strides apart. Make up a straight line sequence during which you pass either over or under your partner's body.

A. Horizontal balances with three points touching the apparatus. Repeat, using only two points touching the apparatus.

Accept any balance when the body is about horizontal. This is difficult work.

In fours

B. Stand in a pattern round a suitable piece of apparatus. Make up a combined group movement which, in general, circles the apparatus but which at certain times moves in towards, on and off and away from the apparatus.

In fours

C. Make a combined balance. Two people on the apparatus and two people using the floor only. Try to make your shape as unusual as possible. Have several attempts at this on different pieces of apparatus.

Balance in fours requires a considerable amount of discussion and, often, amusement. Allow the class to watch some of the better efforts.

In fours

D. Choose a piece of apparatus which is suitable for you to go on and off in cannon. (*Explain.*) Make up an activity which lasts for about half a minute without stopping.

This type of activity needs practising over a period of several lessons. 'In cannon' means one after the other in quick succession.

Children in pairs throughout the lesson.

A. Find five different ways of supporting your partner who is doing a two-point balance on the floor. Make your shape look as spectacular as possible. Stretch arms or legs which are not being used.

B. Make an unusual balance shape with your partner. Now make up a sequence of movements, starting at least five yards away from each other, which is timed to finish with this first balance shape.

This is very challenging. Both partners must arrive at a certain spot simultaneously in order to finish in the balance.

Half class using mats

C. Support your partner who is doing a balance. Gradually reduce this support in order that your partner may roll away. As he rolls away you also complete a roll.

Change

D. A straight-line sequence of leap, weight on hands, roll, working alongside your partner. Keep the same timing as your partner and roll on the same mat.

Two people are usually able to roll on the same mat, if it is used sideways on.

E. Over your partner with a stretch, using him for support. Your partner then does a similar movement, using you for support, and so on.

This can be a vigorous and exciting sequence.